FROM SEA to SHINING SEA

SOUTH CAROLINA

MYRA S. WEATHERLY

Consultants

MELISSA N. MATUSEVICH, PH.D.
Curriculum and Instruction Specialist
Blacksburg, Virginia

ELLEN W. STRINGER
Youth Services Coordinator
Lexington County Public Library System
Lexington, South Carolina

CHILDREN'S PRESS®
A DIVISION OF SCHOLASTIC INC.

New York · Toronto · London · Auckland · Sydney · Mexico City
New Delhi · Hong Kong · ~~Danbury, Connecticut~~

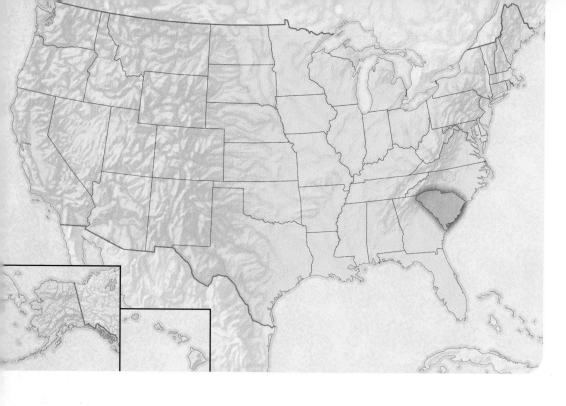

South Carolina is in the southeastern part of the United States. It is bordered by North Carolina, Georgia, and the Atlantic Ocean.

Project Editor: Meredith DeSousa
Art Director: Marie O'Neill
Photo Researcher: Marybeth Kavanagh
Design: Robin West, Ox and Company, Inc.
Page 6 map and recipe art: Susan Hunt Yule
All other maps: XNR Productions, Inc.

Library of Congress Cataloging-in-Publication Data
Weatherly, Myra.
    South Carolina / Myra S. Weatherly.
    p.cm. – (From sea to shining sea)
    Includes bibliographical references (p.) and index.
    ISBN 0-516-22317-8
1. South Carolina—Juvenile literature. [1. South Carolina.] I. Title. II. From sea to shining sea (Series)

F269.3 .W43 2002
975.7—dc21   2001028875

CHAPTER TWO

THE LAND OF SOUTH CAROLINA

On a map, South Carolina looks like a little triangle, or a slice of pie with jagged edges. The state is wedged between North Carolina to the north and Georgia to the south and west. To the east, more than three thousand miles (4,828 kilometers) of Atlantic Ocean stretch between South Carolina and the coast of Africa. Its total area is 32,007 square miles (82,898 square kilometers).

Despite its small size, the Palmetto State abounds with natural beauty. From its sandy beaches to the Blue Ridge Mountains, the landscape of South Carolina varies from one place to the next. You can build sandcastles on the beach and listen to the roar of waterfalls in the mountains.

South Carolina has three natural regions—the Blue Ridge, the Piedmont, and the Atlantic Coastal Plain. South Carolinians call the coastal plains "low country." The Piedmont is sometimes called "upcountry."

South Carolina has more swampland than any other state except Louisiana. Here, a man is canoeing through a cypress swamp.

FIND OUT MORE

Only four states in the country have just two states as neighbors. South Carolina is one. Can you find the other three on a map?

7

THE BLUE RIDGE

The Blue Ridge region gets its name from the Blue Ridge Mountains, which cover the northwestern corner of the state. The Cherokees called the Blue Ridge Mountains *Sahkanga*, meaning "the great blue hills of God." The Blue Ridge Mountains are the eastern range of the Appalachian Mountains, the oldest mountains in North America. This region covers about five hundred square miles (1,295 sq km). Sassafras Mountain, at 3,560 feet (1,085 meters), is the state's highest point. Nearby is Caesar's Head, a huge rock formation that resembles a head. Some people say the mountain was named for Julius Caesar, the ancient Roman leader.

Ancient people left their mark on South Carolina's mountains by carving symbols into the rocks. Scientists believe these rock carvings—

Table Rock State Park is one of the most beautiful parks in the Blue Ridge Mountains.

TABLE of CONTENTS

CHAPTER ONE

INTRODUCING THE PALMETTO STATE

Charleston's distinctive architecture and beautiful palmetto trees make it one of the prettiest cities in the southeast.

South Carolina is the smallest state in the southeastern region of the United States. It is also one of the smallest in the country, ranking fortieth in size. However, its mountains, gardens, beaches, harbors, and islands rank high on beauty, making it one of the loveliest states. Many tourists flock to South Carolina each year to enjoy its beautiful scenery.

South Carolina was one of the original thirteen colonies. In the beginning, North Carolina and South Carolina were one colony, called Carolina, named for King Charles I of England (Carolina is a Latin word for *Charles*). In 1729 they officially separated, and the word *South* was added to its name.

South Carolina's nickname is "the Palmetto State" after the palmetto tree, which grows in the southern part of the state, as well as in other coastal areas of the southeastern United States. It has also been planted widely in Columbia, the state capital. The palmetto tree has played an important part in the history of the state. During the Revolutionary War, colonists defended Charleston harbor from a small fort made of palmetto logs. The palmetto tree is pictured on the state seal and the state flag.

What comes to mind when you think of South Carolina?

- Colonists fighting British soldiers during the American Revolution
- The attack on Fort Sumter, signaling the start of the Civil War
- Tourists strolling along the cobblestone streets in historic Charleston
- People playing golf and tennis on Hilton Head Island
- Stately plantations surrounded by beautiful gardens
- Horse racing at the Aiken Triple Crown and the Carolina Cup
- BMWs rolling off the assembly lines in Greer
- Whitewater rafting on the Chattooga River
- Families enjoying the sun and sand at Myrtle Beach

South Carolina is an old state with a colorful past, known for its smiling faces and beautiful places. Turn the page to discover the fascinating story of South Carolina.

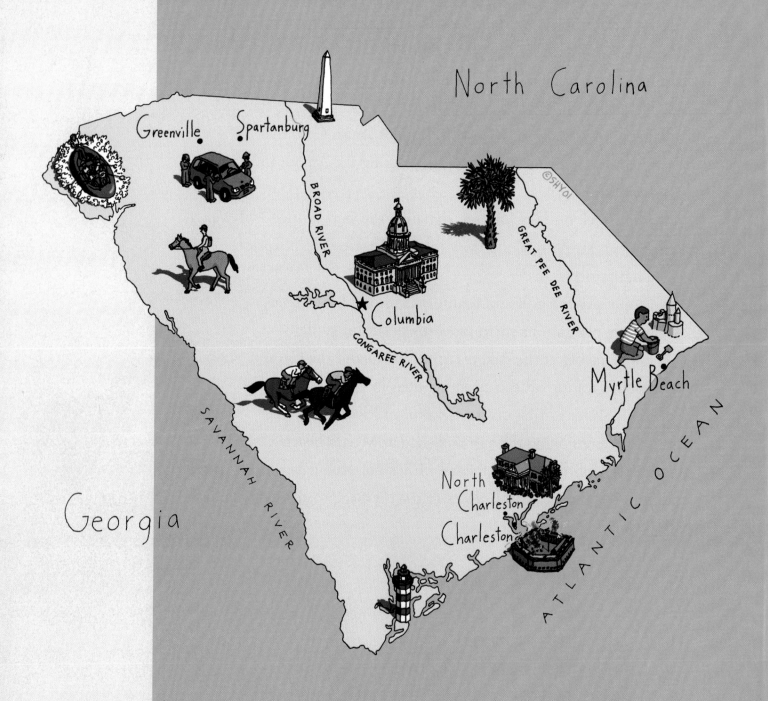

North Carolina

Georgia

Greenville
Spartanburg

BROAD RIVER

GREAT PEE DEE RIVER

Columbia

CONGAREE RIVER

SAVANNAH RIVER

Myrtle Beach

North
Charleston

Charleston

ATLANTIC OCEAN

©SHYOl

in the shapes of circles, ovals, horseshoes, and P-shapes—date back before the time of the Cherokees. In 1990, only six rock carvings had been discovered. Since 1997, hundreds of carvings have been found on remote mountainsides. Today, people are actively searching to locate and record this part of the state's heritage.

There are dozens of beautiful waterfalls in South Carolina's northwest corner. Their white, frothy water tumbles off cliffs into shaded green pools below. One of the most famous is Issaqueena Falls, with a drop of two hundred feet (61 m). Legend says that Issaqueena, a Cherokee maiden, warned settlers of a planned attack by the Cherokees. To escape the anger of her people, she pretended to throw herself from the falls and hid beneath the rushing water. The annual Issaqueena Festival in Six Mile is held in her honor.

One of the highest waterfalls in the eastern United States is Whitewater Falls, located on the border of North and South Carolina. The upper portion of the falls is

FIND OUT MORE

Ancient rock carvings are disappearing at a rapid rate. What might be causing the carvings to disappear?

Whitewater Falls is on the border of North and South Carolina. A section of the falls lies in both states.

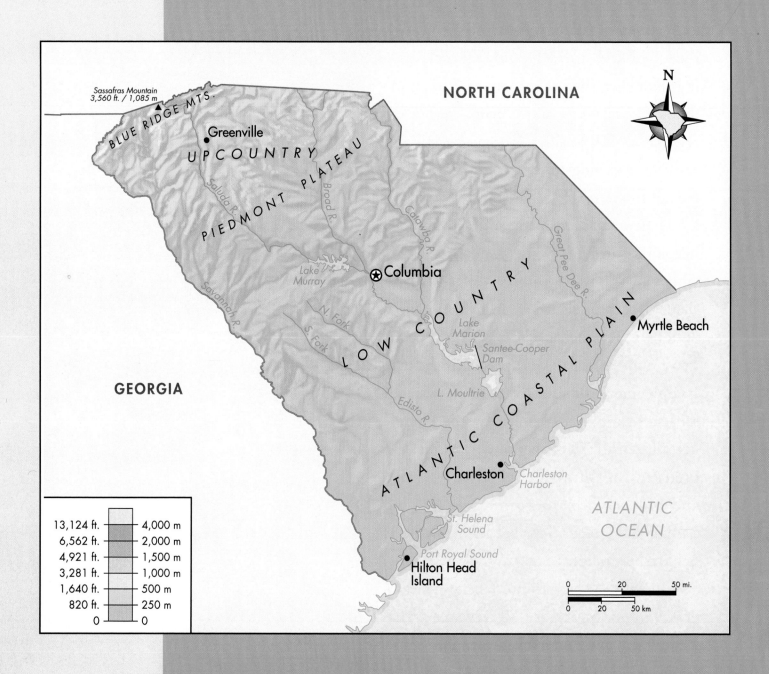

Sassafras Mountain
3,560 ft. / 1,085 m

BLUE RIDGE MTS.

• Greenville

UPCOUNTRY

PIEDMONT PLATEAU

Saluda R.

Broad R.

Catawba R.

NORTH CAROLINA

N

Great Pee Dee R.

Lake
Murray

☆ Columbia

Savannah R.

N. Fork

S. Fork

LOW COUNTRY

Lake
Marion

Santee-Cooper
Dam

• Myrtle Beach

GEORGIA

L. Moultrie

ATLANTIC COASTAL PLAIN

Edisto R.

Charleston •

Charleston
Harbor

ATLANTIC
OCEAN

St. Helena
Sound

Port Royal Sound

• Hilton Head
Island

13,124 ft.   4,000 m
6,562 ft.   2,000 m
4,921 ft.   1,500 m
3,281 ft.   1,000 m
1,640 ft.   500 m
820 ft.   250 m
0   0

0   20   50 mi.
0   20   50 km

in North Carolina, and the lower falls are in South Carolina. Each drop is over four hundred feet (122 m).

From the Blue Ridge Mountain area into the Piedmont to the east, the land drops two thousand feet (610 m) in elevation in only one to two miles (2 to 3 km). Streams have carved gorges (deep narrow passageways) down the sloping land. The Jocassee Gorges, located near Lake Jocassee in northwestern South Carolina, offer beautiful mountain scenery as well as rare plants and a variety of wildlife.

THE PIEDMONT

Next to the Blue Ridge is the Piedmont. Together, these regions cover the northwestern third of the state. The Piedmont is a land of rolling hills dotted with valleys. This region descends gradually from a height of twelve hundred feet (366 m) at the foot of the Blue Ridge Mountains to three hundred feet (91 m) at the fall line. The fall line divides the Piedmont region from the Atlantic Coastal Plain. The land to the west of the fall line is higher than the land to the east, creating waterfalls and river rapids.

More than a hundred years ago, the region's moist red clay was covered by thick layers of topsoil. Many years of farming robbed the soil of nutrients and water wore down the soil to the clay. The 1900s brought better methods of farming, and new crops flourished in the Piedmont. The first peach orchard in South Carolina was planted in the Piedmont in 1901. Today, peaches are still grown here, but factories, houses, golf

The Harbour Town lighthouse is a familiar landmark to Hilton Head's many visitors.

courses, and pastures have replaced many orchards.

ATLANTIC COASTAL PLAIN

The flat and low Atlantic Coastal Plain covers the southeastern two-thirds of the Palmetto State. The western edge of the Atlantic Coastal Plain includes a belt of sand hills. Millions of years ago the ocean covered the plain. These sandy ridges are the dunes of that ancient beach. Some of the sand hills rise up to six hundred feet (183 m).

The part of the Atlantic Coastal Plain that stretches from the sand hills to near the Atlantic Ocean is known as the inner plain. This gently sloping region, with its warm and wet soil, is well suited to farming. In the early days, this was rice and cotton plantation country. Today, tobacco and truck crops, such as tomatoes, melons, and cabbage, are grown here.

The outer coastal plain stretches from the Atlantic Ocean to about fifty miles (80 km) inland. This is an area of low-lying swamps, marshland, beaches, and islands off the coast. South Carolina has more than three hundred miles (483 km) of coastline. Beach resorts dot the white sands. Many islands lie off the coast including Hilton Head, Pawley's, Edisto, and Kiawah Islands.

FIND OUT MORE

The meat-eating Venus's-flytrap is a rare plant that grows in the wetlands of South Carolina. The plant lures flying insects onto its sweet-tasting leaves, then closes its leaves like a trap. How does the Venus's-flytrap get nutrients from the insect?

The loggerhead sea turtle lives on Hilton Head and Isle of Palms. When females reach twenty-five to thirty years old, they return to the beach where they were hatched to lay their eggs. However, the males never return to shore. Beachfront development disrupts the loggerheads' environment, making life hard for them. Today it is against the law to touch a sea turtle.

Loggerhead sea turtles are part of South Carolina's beach wildlife. These turtles can weigh up to 400 pounds (181 kg).

Many of South Carolina's rivers begin in the Blue Ridge Mountains of North Carolina. In the northeastern part of the state, the Pee Dee River flows southeast to the Atlantic Ocean. The Little Pee Dee is a tributary, or a smaller stream, that flows into the Pee Dee. Other major rivers include the Santee, the Broad, and the Saluda. The Broad and Saluda rivers drain much of the north central part of the state. They join to create the Congaree River. The Santee is in lower South Carolina. The Edisto and the Salkehatchie Rivers are in the south. The Savannah River forms South Carolina's border with Georgia.

South Carolina has no large natural lakes. The biggest lakes in the state are manmade. Lake Marion is the largest, covering 110,000 acres (44,515 hectares). Lake Marion is connected to Lake Moultrie by a canal. These lakes are both located in the southern part of the state. Other manmade lakes include Greenwood, Wylie, Murray, Hartwell, and Wateree. Dams on several lakes produce hydroelectric power (electricity generated through the use of water power) for the people of South Carolina.

CLIMATE

Usually, the climate in this southern state is pleasant. Hot summers and mild winters are typical in South Carolina. In June 1954 at Camden, the temperature soared to an all-time high of 111° Fahrenheit (44° Celsius). On a cold day in January 1977, temperatures at Caesar's Head

opposite:
The Combahee River winds its way through South Carolina's forests.

Powerful Hurricane Hugo caused incredible destruction across South Carolina.

plunged to an all-time low of –20°F (–29°C). In the winter, snow often falls in the Blue Ridge Mountains but rarely in other parts of the state. Most of the state's precipitation comes in the form of rain. The average rainfall is about 45 inches (114 centimeters) each year.

Hurricanes, or fierce storms, sometimes strike the southeastern United States, including South Carolina. In September 1989, Hurricane Hugo unleashed its fury on the east coast. Winds and high waters wreaked havoc in Charleston. McClellanville, north of Charleston, was flattened by winds reaching over 130 miles per hour (209 km per hour). The storm lifted roofs, tossed boats around, and snapped trees. Beaches on the Barrier Islands were severely eroded, or washed away. Hurricane Hugo left eighteen people dead and caused $5 billion in property damage in South Carolina.

CHAPTER THREE

SOUTH CAROLINA THROUGH HISTORY

The earliest people arrived in South Carolina at least eleven thousand years ago. They roamed the area, hunting game and gathering roots, nuts, and berries. Recently, scientists have found stone spearheads these people left behind.

About four thousand years ago, these Native Americans began to farm. They planted squash, beans, pumpkins, and corn. They shaped clay into jugs and pots and made clothing out of animal skins. In the coastal areas, they used Spanish moss for baby diapers. Turtle shells became bowls. The children played a type of ball game, using sticks and a deerskin ball.

When the first Europeans arrived in the 1500s, between twenty-five and thirty-five Native American groups lived in South Carolina. The largest groups were the Yamassee, the Catawba, and the Cherokee. The Yamassee lived in the south, near the mouth of the Savannah River.

Colonists worked hard building homes and starting farms to make the Carolina colony successful.

FIND OUT MORE

Millions of years ago, the eastern half of South Carolina was under the Atlantic Ocean. Today, many fossils—traces of plants and animals from long ago—have been found in South Carolina. Seashells and sharks' teeth have been unearthed in the sand hills, a long way from the present seashore. Find out what other types of fossils have been found, and what clues they give us about the kind of animals that once lived in the state.

They spoke Muskogee, the language of the Creeks. They used bark, grass, and palmetto leaves to build their homes.

The Catawba lived in the northeastern part of the state, along the banks of the Catawba River. They settled in villages, and built their homes in oval or round shapes, using bent saplings and bark.

This drawing by John White shows an early Native American village in the South Carolina area.

The Cherokee lived in the foothills of the Blue Ridge Mountains, in villages surrounded by log walls. They used deerskins for clothing. The men hunted bear, deer, and other wild animals, and the villagers farmed corn, beans, squash, and melons. The Cherokee belonged to the Iroquoian language group. Other Native American groups included the Waccamaw, the Santee, and the Cusabo.

EUROPEAN EXPLORATION

In 1521, a Spanish ship with tall sails stopped at Winyah Bay on the coast of South Carolina. The captain, Francisco Gordillo, tricked the Native Americans by inviting them on board, then holding them as prisoners. The Spaniards sailed from South Carolina to the West Indies with more than one hundred prisoners.

One of Gordillo's captives, Chicora, learned Spanish and entertained the Spaniards with wild tales. He said his homeland was rich in gold. Inspired by Chicora's fanciful tales, Spaniard Lucas Vásquez de Ayllón led a fleet of three ships back to Winyah Bay in 1526. He brought five hundred men, women, and children, 89 horses, and tools for starting a colony. Ayllón founded South Carolina's first European settlement near present-day Georgetown. It didn't last long. After a few months, two out of every three colonists died from starvation and illness. The surviving settlers returned to the West Indies.

In 1562, the French started a settlement on Parris Island. When the expected supply ships did not arrive, the French soldiers left their fort and set sail for France in a homemade boat. The failure of the Spanish and French paved the way for English settlement.

ENGLISH SETTLEMENT

In 1607, England established a colony at Jamestown, Virginia. England's King Charles I named the region south of Virginia *Carolana* (Land of Charles), later called *Carolina*. In 1670, the first group of English colonists—148 men and women—arrived on the Carolina coast. They came from the English colony of Barbados in the Caribbean Sea. Their settlement on the Ashley River was called Charles Town. Ten years later, the settlement moved to its present site. It eventually was renamed Charleston.

The first settlers were farmers and traders. They planted cottonseed, sugarcane, and vegetables. They traded tools, rum, and guns with Native Americans in exchange for deerskins and animal furs. Animal pelts, which were especially valuable in England, were shipped there and sold.

In 1671, more settlers arrived from Barbados. They started large farms called plantations. Plantations required many workers, so Africans were brought into the colony and put to work as slaves. Slaves lived in harsh conditions and were often treated poorly by their owners. They did not have the freedom to go wherever they wanted, and were punished for trying to escape. Over the next two years, half of the settlers and more than half of the captured Africans came from Barbados.

opposite:
Colonist John Boone and his family lived in Boone Hall during the late 1600s and early 1700s. It became an important cotton plantation, covering thousands of acres.

Around 1680, rice was introduced to the colony. Slaves taught their masters the African way to successfully grow rice in the swampy coastal lands. Vast rice crops brought wealth to the planters.

Indigo, a plant used to make blue dye, was another money-making crop. In colonial times, blue was a valuable color, having been previously worn only by kings and queens. The first attempts to grow indigo failed. In 1739, teenager Eliza Lucas received indigo seeds from her father in the West Indies. Her first attempt to grow indigo was not successful, and in a letter to her father she wrote: "Perhaps the plants were harvested too soon or the temperature in the vats was not just right . . . I want to try again. . . ." After five years of trying, Eliza successfully produced blue dye from indigo. With her help, other planters began to grow indigo. Soon it became a major export to England.

The colony flourished. In 1712, Carolina was divided into two parts, North and South. Both North and South Carolina officially became separate colonies of England in 1729. During the mid-1700s, more settlers came to South Carolina. People from Pennsylvania, Virginia, and New York settled in the upcountry. Many of the European settlers were from Scotland. These people owned small farms and had little need for slaves.

As the colonies grew, settlers began taking land that belonged to Native Americans. The Yamassee and other Native American tribes became angry. Not only were they losing precious land, their people were also ravaged by diseases brought on by the settlers. In 1715, war broke out between Native American warriors and the colonists. At one plantation, the Yamassee killed one hundred settlers, but Native

American losses were much greater. In the end, the colonists won the war and drove most of the Yamassee south of the Savannah River.

Pirates were another danger to colonial life. They robbed ships along the Carolina coast. Edward Teach, called Blackbeard, was a well-known pirate. In May 1718, he blocked ships from going in or out of Charleston Harbor, threatening to burn the city unless his demands were met. What Blackbeard demanded was not gold or silver, but medicine for his sick men. The city delivered a chest of medicine and Blackbeard retreated to North Carolina.

Another pirate, Stede Bonnet, was a wealthy man from Barbados. For a time, Bonnet and his fleet sailed with Blackbeard. In November of 1718, Bonnet and his crew were captured and later hanged at Charleston.

Blackbeard was one of the most feared pirates along the Carolina coast.

EXTRA! EXTRA!

Not all pirates were men. Anne Bonny, daughter of a wealthy merchant, grew up in Charleston. At age sixteen, she ran away from home and became a pirate. She was later captured and sentenced to be hanged. However, Anne escaped the hangman's noose because she was pregnant. It is said that her father eventually paid money for her return to the Carolinas, where she assumed a new name and a new life.

Colonial Charleston was a major slave trading port for all of the thirteen colonies.

By 1720, South Carolina's African slaves outnumbered the colonists. Slaves' harsh living and working conditions often led to runaways and rebellions. In 1739, a group of slaves broke into a store at Stono Bridge, twenty miles (32 km) southwest of Charleston. The rebels murdered the owners and stole firearms, crying out for "liberty!" They killed several settlers before they were stopped by a group of armed white men. The Stono Rebellion, as it was called, left about sixty slaves and twenty-five settlers dead.

THE AMERICAN REVOLUTION

In the 1770s, England needed money. To help raise money, England placed taxes (extra charges) on certain goods such as glass, paper, and tea. Many colonists thought the taxes were unfair, and rebels throughout the colonies led protests against England. They destroyed cartons of tea to protest the Tea Act, and started riots in response to the Stamp Act. The colonists resented being governed by a ruler almost 3,000 miles (4,828 km) away. They wanted independence from England.

England, however, didn't want to let the colonies go. In 1775, the American Revolution (1775–1783) broke out. British troops came from England to fight against the colonists. On June 28, 1776, English ships attacked a palmetto log fort, later named Fort Moultrie, on Sullivan's Island in Charleston Harbor. The enemy's cannonballs sank into the soft palmetto logs with a dull thud, causing little damage to the fort. The battle ended with the British in defeat.

Six days later, on July 4, 1776, leaders from the thirteen colonies signed a document called the Declaration of Independence. This

Fort Moultrie was used during both the American Revolution and the Civil War. The fort was rebuilt twice, after being destroyed by hurricanes in 1783 and 1804.

WHO'S WHO IN SOUTH CAROLINA?

Francis Marion (1732–1795) was a famous soldier during the American Revolution. The tricks he used against the British army earned him the nickname "Swamp Fox." Using speed and surprise, the barely five-foot (2 m) tall Marion and his men would emerge from the swamps and strike. Then, they disappeared into the marshes. A British officer once said, "The devil himself could not catch that old fox in these swamps." After the war, Francis served in the state senate. He was born on a farm near Charleston.

important document gave reasons why the colonies should be independent from England. Four men—Edward Rutledge, Thomas Heyward Jr., Thomas Lynch Jr., and Arthur Middleton—signed the Declaration of Independence on behalf of South Carolina.

Because declaring freedom and actually being free are quite different, the war raged on throughout the colonies until 1783. Almost two hundred battles took place in South Carolina, more battles than occurred in any other colony. About 25,000 South Carolinians fought in the war. Not all South Carolinians, however, fought against the English—some people fought for England.

In 1780, the British attacked Charleston again. After capturing the city, British troops marched inland where they encountered surprise attacks. Troops of colonists hid in the swamps and ambushed the British when they least expected an attack. The most famous of these soldiers was Francis Marion. Another great leader was

Thomas Sumter. He led surprise raids against the British in central South Carolina. He was such a fierce fighter that he was called "the Gamecock," after the fighting rooster known for its spirit and courage.

A colonial victory at Kings Mountain in 1780 helped change the tide of the war. Another important success was the Battle of Cowpens in 1781, which was won with the help of soldier Andrew Pickens. Against all odds, the colonists' ragtag army defeated the world's strongest nation. With the signing of the peace treaty in 1783, the thirteen colonies were free to form their own government.

South Carolina became the eighth state of the United States on May 23, 1788. In 1790, the state capital was moved from Charleston to Columbia, a planned capital city in the center of the state.

Most plantation owners couldn't do without a cotton gin, which made cotton production faster and easier.

STATEHOOD

After the war, South Carolina continued to grow. Cotton replaced rice and indigo as South Carolina's main crop. At first, removing seed from the short fibers was difficult and time-consuming. The invention of the cotton gin in 1793 made cotton production faster and cheaper. This machine separated the seeds from the cotton fibers fifty times faster than a person could do it. Cotton production moved to the upcountry.

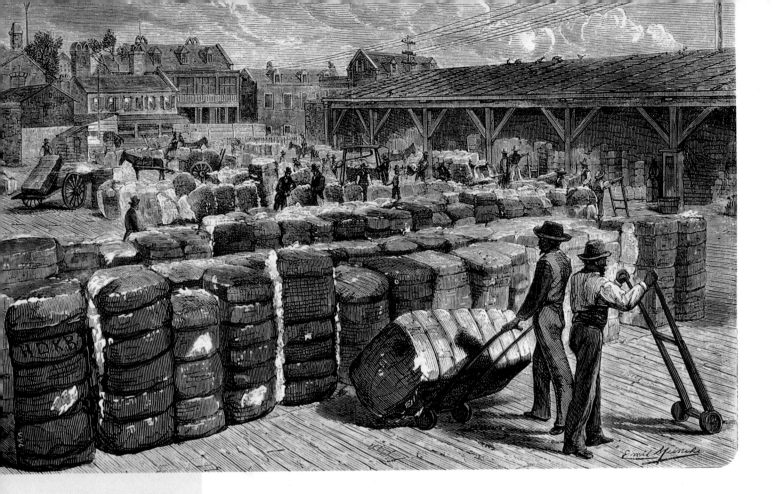

Busy cotton wharfs like this one turned Charleston into an important colonial seaport by the mid-1700s.

Cotton was big business. Piedmont farmers became plantation owners who used slave labor. By 1850, South Carolina had 400,000 slaves. This was more than half the state's total population.

While slavery was common in the southern states, most Northerners were against it. As the young country grew, North and South developed in different ways. In the South, farming was the main way of life. Their large plantations could only be run with the help of slaves. In the North, factories and businesses employed people and paid them wages. Slavery was illegal in the North.

In the early 1800s, a movement to end slavery started in the North.

Southerners felt that it should be left up to each state to decide whether or not to own slaves. The leading speaker for slavery and states' rights was South Carolinian John C. Calhoun. President Andrew Jackson strongly opposed Calhoun's views. In South Carolina, Joel Robert Poinsett led a group called the Unionists, who were also against Calhoun's ideas. Charleston-born sisters Angelina and Sarah Grimké spoke out about the evils of slavery. They traveled throughout the northeast, urging women to help overthrow slavery.

When Abraham Lincoln was elected president of the United States in 1860, southerners feared he would free the slaves. As a result, many southern states seceded (withdrew) from the Union and formed a new nation called the Confederate States of America. South Carolina was the first to secede on December 20, 1860. Ten other southern states followed.

WHO'S WHO IN SOUTH CAROLINA?

John C. Calhoun (1782–1850) served in South Carolina's legislature and in the federal government as a United States congressman, secretary of war, and secretary of state. He also served as vice president under Andrew Jackson. Ultimately, he resigned from his post as vice president because he disagreed with some of Jackson's ideas. He was born in Abbeville.

WHO'S WHO IN SOUTH CAROLINA?

Joel Robert Poinsett (1779–1851) was the first United States ambassador to Mexico. In 1825 he returned from a trip to Mexico with a flowering plant that bloomed during winter months. The plant was named "Poinsettia" in honor of Poinsett. He was born in Charleston.

FAMOUS FIRSTS

- The first opera performed in America was in Charleston, 1735
- The first shot fired in the Civil War was on Fort Sumter, April 12, 1861
- Columbia Mill was the world's first totally electric textile mill, 1893
- The first cotton mill was built on James Island, 1789
- The Charleston Museum was America's first public museum, founded in 1773
- The first public library was established in Charleston, 1698
- The "Best Friend of Charleston" was the first steam locomotive built for regular passenger service, 1830

THE CIVIL WAR

The first clash of the Civil War (1861–1865) took place in Charleston Harbor on April 12, 1861. Confederate soldiers fired on Fort Sumter, a United States fort. People in Charleston crowded housetops and church steeples to watch what looked like a huge fireworks display. The shelling continued for 34 hours. Finally, the Union soldiers surrendered.

The first sinking of a warship by a submarine occurred on February 17, 1864. The H.L. Hunley—a Confederate submarine that looked

like a big tin can—sank a Union ship in Charleston Harbor. Mysteriously, the Hunley and its crew disappeared.

South Carolinians suffered greatly during the Civil War. Union ships blocked Charleston trade. In 1865 Columbia and other parts of South Carolina suffered a huge blow when Union General William T. Sherman marched through the state, burning plantations and the city of Columbia. Teenager Emma LeConte wrote about the burning of Columbia in her diary. "Imagine night turned into noonday, only with a blazing, scorching glare that was horrible. . . . On every side the crackling and devouring fire, while every instant came the crashing of timbers and the thunder of falling buildings." Nearly 65,000 South Carolinians fought in the war. By the time Confederate forces surrendered on April 9, 1865, about 15,000 of the state's soldiers had died in battle.

THE RECONSTRUCTION ERA

After the war, the defeated southern states began rebuilding. This era was known as Reconstruction. South Carolina's economy was in ruins. Slaves were declared free as a result of the war, and without slave labor the plantation system broke down. While some plantation owners continued to run their businesses, others abandoned their property and

opposite:
Fort Sumter endured attacks for almost two years during the Civil War, reducing most of the fort to brick rubble.

moved out of South Carolina. Most of the freed slaves (freedmen) had no money, no homes, and no jobs.

Many small farmers and freedmen became sharecroppers. Sharecroppers did not own the land they farmed. Instead, they farmed someone else's land, but were required to share their crops with the landowner. They were also charged extra money for the use of tools and seeds. This system made it difficult for sharecroppers to make a profit.

With the adoption of a new state constitution, South Carolina was allowed to rejoin the United States in June 1868. African-American men were given the right to vote and hold office. Some African-Americans served in the legislature.

However, in later years, whites began to block improvements for African-Americans. Groups such as the Ku Klux Klan (KKK) terrorized and killed African-Americans all over the South. In South Carolina, a group called the Red Shirts tried to control blacks in an effort to prevent them from using their new-found freedoms. A new state constitution, adopted in 1895, prevented most African-Americans from voting. Also, a series of "Jim Crow" laws created segregation, or separation, of blacks and whites. African-Americans were required to use separate restrooms, railroad cars, drinking fountains, and schools. Some places allowed whites

WHAT'S IN A NAME?

Many names of places in South Carolina have interesting origins.

Name	Comes from or means
Carolina	King Charles I of England
Georgetown	King George II
Pee Dee River	Native American group who lived on its banks
Hilton Head Island	William Hilton, English sea captain
Francis Marion National Forest	Francis Marion
Sumter National Forest	Thomas Sumter

only. Buses required African-Americans to sit at the back of the bus. These laws were a huge setback for African-Americans, making it clear that whites did not view them as equal.

GROWTH AND CHANGE

The textile industry was booming in the late 1880s. Because of the huge amounts of cotton grown in the state, the industry grew quickly. Also, many textile mills in the north moved to the "New South" to take advantage of cheap labor. By 1905, almost 40,000 men, women, and children worked in the textile mills of Anderson, Spartanburg, and Greenville counties alone.

However, wages were low and workers could barely afford what they

This woman is working on a mechanical loom in a cotton mill.

needed to live. They had no choice but to live in company-owned mill towns. The company did not own only the mill, but it also owned the grocery store and the workers' homes. Some mills issued brass coins that could be used only in company stores. This situation often allowed businesses to take advantage of workers by charging high rents and requiring long working hours, for children as well as men and women.

During World War I (1914–1918), soldiers trained at Camp Jackson in Columbia, Camp Sevier in Greenville, and Camp Wadsworth outside

Spartanburg. Also, the state's textile mills produced large quantities of cloth for the armed forces. South Carolina textile mills refused to hire African-Americans, however. Looking for factory work, many African-Americans moved North, where businesses were willing to give them jobs. The 1930 state census showed whites outnumbering African-Americans for the first time in 120 years.

In 1921, cotton prices fell. The same year, insects called boll weevils destroyed half the state's cotton crop by devouring the fibers and seeds inside the boll. Farmers began growing tobacco, soybeans, peaches, wheat, and corn to replace cotton. Many farmers left their farms to work in cities.

In the 1920s, many people invested money in the stock market, which gave them a piece of ownership in various companies and businesses. In 1929, the stock market plunged and people all around the country lost money as a result of their investments. This was the start of what became known as the Great Depression (1929–1939). Businesses weren't able to sell enough products because people could no longer afford to buy things. In South Carolina, mills closed. Farm prices tumbled. Banks and other businesses shut down. Thousands of South Carolina textile workers lost their jobs, and others worked for such low wages they could barely buy food and pay for their homes.

It wasn't until the start of World War II (1939–1945) that the Great Depression gradually came to an end. Farm prices recovered, and textile

Boll weevils destroyed much of the state's cotton crop in 1921.

mills operated around the clock, making cloth for military uniforms. Wartime industries opened in the state as well as bases for training the armed forces. Marines trained at Parris Island, and Charleston Navy Yard served as an important base for warships.

MODERN TIMES

Starting in the 1950s, African-Americans in South Carolina slowly began regaining their rights. In 1948, African-Americans were allowed to vote. In the 1950s, better schools—but still separate—were provided for African-Americans. In 1954, the United States Supreme Court ruled that having separate schools for whites and blacks is against the United States Constitution. However, South Carolina and other southern states ignored the ruling for many years.

In 1964, the Civil Rights Act required racial integration, which forced South Carolina and other states to end school segregation. South Carolina still resisted. It wasn't until 1970 that South Carolina's public schools were attended by students of all races. Since many of South Carolina's neighborhoods were either primarily African-American or primarily white, it was necessary to bus children from one neighborhood school to another in order to have racial balance. Today, South Carolina is focused on improving the quality of education for all children in the state.

WHO'S WHO IN SOUTH CAROLINA?

Harvey Gantt (1943–) was the first African-American to enroll at a public university in South Carolina. He entered Clemson University in January 1963, after a federal court ordered the all-white college to admit him. Gantt graduated in 1965 with a degree in architecture. He was born in Charleston.

Beginning in the 1970s, cheap labor lured many companies from Japan, West Germany, France, Holland, and other countries to South Carolina. From 1998 to 2000, more than 60,000 new jobs were created. In 2000, over 255 international factories were located here. In contrast, the number of farmers has gone down in recent years. By 1980, only about four of every one hundred jobs in the state were on farms, compared to five of ten jobs in 1940.

Controversy arose in South Carolina as recently as the year 2000. For years, the State House in Columbia displayed three flags—the flag of the United States of America, the flag of South Carolina, and a flag showing the "Southern Cross" based on the battle jack carried by

Since most neighborhoods were primarily either white or black, many students were bussed from one neighborhood to another to end school segregation.

The "Rebel flag," removed from the State House dome, now flies near a Confederate soldier's memorial on the State House lawn.

Confederate troops during the Civil War. Some people in South Carolina felt that the flag symbolizing the Confederacy should be removed because they see it as a symbol of slavery. Many others, however, view it as a symbol of southern heritage, to honor people who fought for the Confederacy during the Civil War.

South Carolinians participated in debates and protests regarding the flag. Finally, the state legislature took a vote and decided to remove the flag from the dome. On July 1, 2000, the Confederate flag that had fluttered on top of the dome for 38 years came down. Instead, a small Confederate flag is located on the capitol grounds.

South Carolinians are proud of their historic sites and symbols and continually strive to protect their heritage. At the same time, they create a better future for themselves by improving the state's education, industry, and environment. South Carolina faces a bright future in the twenty-first century.

CHAPTER FOUR

GOVERNING SOUTH CAROLINA

South Carolina's government is organized according to its consti-tution. A constitution is a document that outlines the basic laws and principles under which the state is governed. South Carolina has had seven constitutions. The first one was written in 1776. The next six constitutions were adopted in 1778, 1790, 1861, 1865, 1868, and 1895. Today, the state uses the constitution created in 1895. It has been amended (changed) hundreds of times because the people's views of government have changed throughout history.

South Carolina's government is organized in the same way as the United States government. It is divided into three branches, or parts—the executive, legislative, and judicial. Together, these branches govern the state by creating laws, enforcing the laws, and interpreting the laws. None of these branches is more powerful than any other. Instead, they create a balance of power.

The South Carolina State House took 56 years to complete.

EXECUTIVE BRANCH

The job of the executive branch is to enforce and carry out the state's laws. The governor is the head of the executive branch. He or she is elected by the people to serve a four-year term and may be elected again for four more years. The governor promotes industry and tourism for the state, and also recommends a budget, which determines how the state's money will be spent—whether on education, roads, or other things. The governor may also veto a new law that is proposed by the legislature (South Carolina's lawmaking body) by refusing to sign it into law. However, the law can still be passed if two-thirds of the legislature vote to override the governor's veto.

Other people in the executive branch are the lieutenant governor, attorney general, state treasurer, and comptroller general. These people are all elected officials. Many people also work in state agencies, such as the Departments of Agriculture, Transportation, and Education.

LEGISLATIVE BRANCH

The legislative branch makes the laws of the state, such as changing the speed limit on highways or creating a state lottery. Legislators also work on the state budget with the governor. South Carolina's legislature is called the General Assembly. The General Assembly is divided into two branches, or houses: the senate and the house of representatives. The people of South Carolina elect 46 senators for four-year terms and 124 representatives for two-year terms.

JUDICIAL BRANCH

The judicial branch interprets the state's laws in order to resolve disputes. They also determine if the laws are fair. Courts and judges make up the judicial branch.

There are different levels of courts. Trial courts, at the lowest level, hear many different types of cases, such as criminal cases (where someone breaks the law) and civil cases (legal disagreements between people or organizations). If a person is not satisfied with the decision of a trial court, he or she can bring the case to a higher court called the court of appeals.

The supreme court is the highest court in South Carolina. If a case is disputed in appeals court, the supreme court makes the final decision. Four justices and a chief justice serve ten-year terms on the supreme court. Judges are elected by the General Assembly.

TAKE A TOUR OF COLUMBIA, THE STATE CAPITAL

Columbia is South Carolina's largest city. Yet, with more than 115,000 people, Columbia still holds a certain charm. Its combination of rich history and bustling industry makes Columbia an exciting place in the heart of the South.

The capitol building, called the State House, is in the center of downtown Columbia. Construction on the State House began in 1855 and was completed more than fifty years later. Six bronze stars on the west wall mark the spots where Union cannonballs hit the unfinished

WHO'S WHO IN SOUTH CAROLINA?

Jean Toal (1943–) became the first female chief justice to serve on the South Carolina Supreme Court on March 23, 2000. She was born in Columbia.

41

The State House lobby features stained glass windows, beautiful carvings, and an interior view of the dome.

building during the Civil War. Because the massive columns were lying on the ground at the time, they survived the burning of Columbia. The granite building is 180 feet (55 m) tall and has a dome made of copper.

While much of Columbia was destroyed in 1865, there are several buildings throughout the city that remained standing and can be visited today. The Robert Mills House was designed in 1823 by Robert Mills, who also designed the Washington Monument in Washington, D.C.

SOUTH CAROLINA GOVERNORS

Name	Term	Name	Term
*John Rutledge	1776–1778	Benjamin F. Perry	1865
*Rawlins Lowndes	1778–1779	James L. Orr	1865–1868
John Rutledge	1779–1782	Robert K. Scott	1868–1872
John Mathews	1782–1783	Franklin J. Moses, Jr.	1872–1874
Benjamin Guerard	1783–1785	Daniel H. Chamberlain	1874–1876
William Moultrie	1785–1787	Wade Hampton	1876–1879
Thomas Pinckney	1787–1789	William D. Simpson	1879–1880
Charles Pinckney	1789–1792	Thomas B. Jeter	1880
William Moultrie	1792–1794	Johnson Hagood	1880–1882
Arnoldus Vaner Horst	1794–1796	Hugh S. Thompson	1882–1886
Charles Pinckney	1796–1798	John C. Sheppard	1886
Edward Rutledge	1798–1800	John P. Richardson	1886–1890
John Drayton	1800–1802	Benjamin R. Tillman	1890–1894
James B. Richardson	1802–1804	John G. Evans	1894–1897
Paul Hamilton	1804–1806	William H. Ellerbe	1897–1899
Charles Pinckney	1806–1808	Miles B. McSweeney	1899–1903
John Drayton	1808–1810	Duncan C. Heyward	1903–1907
Henry Middleton	1810–1812	Martin F. Ansel	1907–1911
Joseph Alston	1812–1814	Coleman L. Blease	1911–1915
David R. Williams	1814–1816	Charles A. Smith	1915
Andrew Pickens	1816–1818	Richard I. Manning	1915–1919
John Geddes	1818–1820	Robert A. Cooper	1919–1922
Thomas Bennett	1820–1822	Wilson G. Harvey	1922–1923
John L. Wilson	1822–1824	Thomas G. McLeod	1923–1927
Richard I. Manning	1824–1826	John G. Richards	1927–1931
John Taylor	1826–1828	Ibra C. Blackwood	1931–1935
Stephen D. Miller	1828–1830	Olin D. Johnston	1935–1939
James Hamilton, Jr.	1830–1832	Burnet R. Maybank	1939–1941
Robert Y. Hayne	1832–1834	J. Emile Harley	1941–1942
George McDuffie	1834–1836	Richard M. Jeffries	1942–1943
Pierce M. Butler	1836–1838	Olin D. Johnston	1943–1945
Patrick Noble	1838–1840	Ransome J. Williams	1945–1947
B.K. Henagan	1840	Strom Thurmond	1947–1951
John P. Richardson	1840–1842	James F. Byrnes	1951–1955
James H. Hammond	1842–1844	George B. Timmerman, Jr.	1955–1959
William Aiken	1844–1846	Ernest F. Hollings	1959–1963
David Johnson	1846–1848	Donald S. Russell	1963–1965
Whitemarsh B. Seabrook	1848–1850	Robert E. McNair	1965–1971
John H. Means	1850–1852	John C. West	1971–1975
John L. Manning	1852–1854	James B. Edwards	1975–1979
James H. Adams	1854–1856	Richard W. Riley	1979–1987
Robert F.W. Allston	1856–1858	Carroll A. Campbell, Jr.	1987–1995
William H. Gist	1858–1860	David Beaseley	1995–1999
Francis W. Pickens	1860–1862	Jim Hodges	1999–
Milledge L. Bonham	1862–1864		
Andrew G. Magrath	1864–1865	*The governor was called president.	

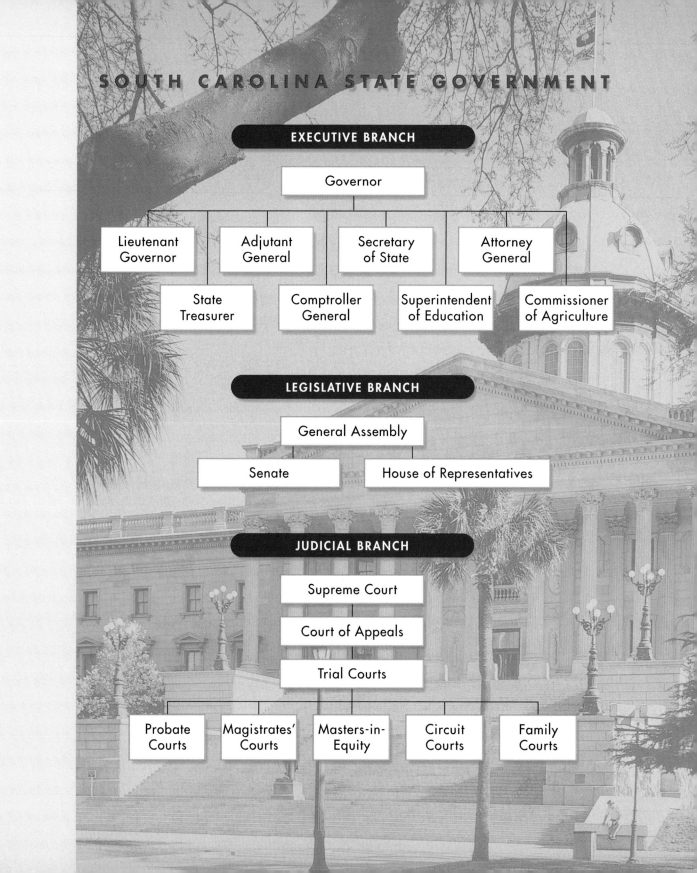

SOUTH CAROLINA STATE GOVERNMENT

EXECUTIVE BRANCH

Governor

- Lieutenant Governor
- Adjutant General
- Secretary of State
- Attorney General
- State Treasurer
- Comptroller General
- Superintendent of Education
- Commissioner of Agriculture

LEGISLATIVE BRANCH

General Assembly

- Senate
- House of Representatives

JUDICIAL BRANCH

Supreme Court

Court of Appeals

Trial Courts

- Probate Courts
- Magistrates' Courts
- Masters-in-Equity
- Circuit Courts
- Family Courts

Beautiful gardens surround the house, including a maze made entirely from boxwood shrubs. The Governor's Mansion, built in 1855, was originally part of a military academy. The academy burned during the Civil War, but the house survived.

Other historic buildings include the Mann-Simons Cottage, home of Celia Mann. Celia Mann was a free African-American who walked

The Mann-Simons cottage is now a museum that houses objects from Columbia's early African-American community.

from Charleston all the way to Columbia to begin a new life. Her home in Columbia often served as a meeting place for church groups in the African-American community. The Woodrow Wilson Boyhood Home houses items pertaining to our 28th president, who lived here as a teenager.

At Riverbanks Zoo, named one of the "10 Great Zoos in America," more than two thousand animals live in their natural surroundings.

Zookeepers feed sea lions at the Riverbanks Zoo.

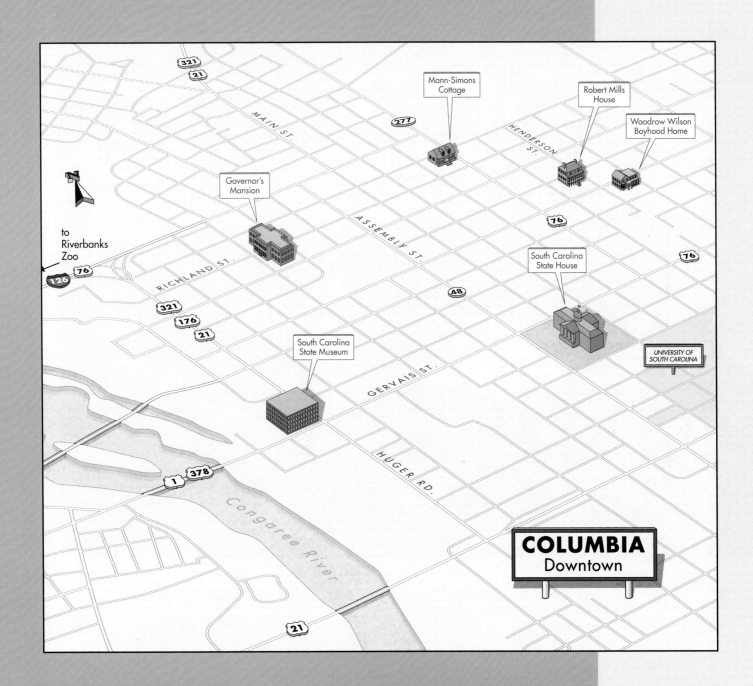

Mann-Simons
Cottage

Robert Mills
House

Woodrow Wilson
Boyhood Home

Governor's
Mansion

to Riverbanks
Zoo

South Carolina
State House

South Carolina
State Museum

UNIVERSITY OF
SOUTH CAROLINA

MAIN ST.

HENDERSON ST.

ASSEMBLY ST.

RICHLAND ST.

GERVAIS ST.

HUGER RD.

Congaree River

321
21
277
76
76
48
126
76
321
176
21
1 378
21

COLUMBIA
Downtown

You'll find seafaring creatures, African lions, giraffes, rhinos, hippos, Siberian tigers, and gorillas. Two of the highlights of the zoo are the chattering monkeys and the sea lion show.

You can learn the story of South Carolina at the South Carolina State

Museum. Hundreds of exhibits celebrate the art, history, science, and technology of the state. The museum itself is located in the old Columbia Mill, dating back to 1893. Some of the exhibits include dinosaur fossils and a life-size reconstruction of a mastodon, a distant relative of today's elephant. You can also see what a radio broadcasting studio looked like in the 1940s.

Columbia is the educational center of the state. The University of South Carolina is the largest university, with more than thirty thousand students. Columbia College, Columbia International University, Benedict College, and Allen University are also located here.

opposite:
In 1833, a train called the "Best Friend of Charleston" ran on a rail line from Charleston to Hamburg. At that time it was the longest rail line in the world. One of the train cars is on display at the South Carolina State Museum.

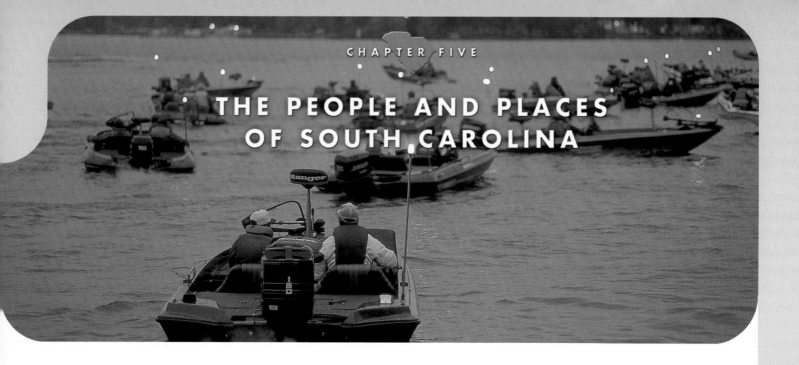

THE PEOPLE AND PLACES OF SOUTH CAROLINA

These people are getting an early-morning start for a fishing tournament on the Santee River.

Scenic beauty and history surround South Carolina. More than twelve hundred historical sites throughout the state are listed on the National Register of Historic Places, our country's official list of important sites that have helped shape the history of the United States. South Carolinians are proud of their state's heritage and enjoy sharing it with others through festivals and other events.

More than three hundred festivals are held throughout the year around the state. Many of these events include music. Myrtle Beach hosts the four-day South Carolina Bluegrass Festival. Charleston's famous international Spoleto Festival includes opera, symphonic music, jazz, dance, theater, and

WHO'S WHO IN SOUTH CAROLINA?

Joseph P. Riley, Jr. (1941–) has been the mayor of Charleston since 1975. He is considered one of the most effective government leaders in America. He has received many awards, including the first President's Award from the United States Conference of Mayors and the Outstanding Mayor's Award. Today, Charleston is recognized as one of the most livable and progressive cities in the country.

puppet shows. This three-week spring event ends with a dazzling display of fireworks.

Other events celebrate cultural features that make the area special. The city of Beaufort hosts an annual Shrimp Festival. To experience the German culture, check out Octoberfest in Walhalla, where you'll find German foods, bands, and dances as well as carnival and hot-air balloon rides. To top it all off, Gaffney's South Carolina Peach Festival features ten days of family fun and entertainment.

MEET THE PEOPLE

More than four million people live in South Carolina. There are about a half million more people living in the state today than in 1990, and more newcomers are arriving every day. South Carolina attracts

Performers from around the world, like these dancers from Cuba, come to Charleston to participate in the Spoleto Festival.

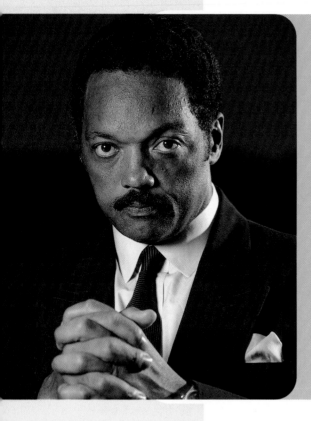

FIND OUT MORE

Using the most recent census figures for South Carolina (www.census.gov/), answer the following questions:

1. Compare South Carolina's population to the population of the United States. How many people live outside South Carolina?
2. Compare South Carolina's land area to the land area of the entire United States. How much of the United States' land area lies outside of South Carolina?
3. What is the most populated city or town in South Carolina? What is the least populated?

older people from northern states. Also, many of the state's residents were born elsewhere or have parents who were born elsewhere, such as Germany and the United Kingdom.

According to the 2000 census, almost seven of every ten South Carolinians are of European descent. About three of every ten people are African-American, two of every hundred people are Hispanic, and one of every hundred people is either Asian or Native American. Most of the 8,000 Native Americans living in South Carolina belong to the Catawba Nation near Rock Hill. The Hispanic population has tripled since the 1990 census.

Another group of people, called Gullah, live on the sea islands of South Carolina. Centuries ago, their ancestors were brought to the islands from Sierra Leone in West

Africa. Before the 1900s, the only way to reach the islands was by boat. Because they were isolated from the rest of society, the sea islands flourished with a unique culture, including art, food, music, and even language. They spoke a special language called Gullah—a blend of English and African words.

Today, bridges and roads connect the Gullah to the mainstream of South Carolina. Outsiders have bought land on the islands to build resorts and homes. Fifty years ago, residents on world-famous Hilton Head Island were almost entirely African-American. Caucasians now outnumber African-Americans by more than eight to one. About 25,000 Gullah people live along the coastal region of South Carolina. The annual Gullah Festival honors and celebrates their heritage.

African dance and drumming is part of the Gullah Festival, an annual five-day celebration in Beaufort.

Before 1980, most South Carolinians lived in rural areas. Now, about five out of ten people live in suburban communities, on the outskirts of large cities, and near South Carolina's beaches. Although the Charleston-North Charleston region gained few people in the last ten years, it is still one of the three largest centers of population, along with Columbia and the Greenville-Spartanburg region.

WORKING IN SOUTH CAROLINA

During its first century of statehood, South Carolina was primarily a farming state and cotton was the main crop. In 1997, of more than two million workers, only two of every hundred people were farmers. Many of the state's twenty thousand farms grow tobacco, which is today's leading crop, as well as soybeans and corn. Some farms raise beef and dairy cattle. Shrubs, flowers, and plants are also grown in nurseries throughout South Carolina.

South Carolinians have worked in manufacturing since the late 1800s. Today, about

seventeen out of every hundred workers are employed in the manufacturing industry. Chemicals head the list of manufactured products, followed by textiles and machinery. Factories in Charleston, Spartanburg, and Greenville produce chemicals, and one of the leading chemical companies in the world, BASF, has a site in Anderson. Paper and paper products are the state's fourth leading manufactured products. Factories in Greenville and Rock Hill produce paper goods. A huge plant in Hartsville produces plastic bags. Other large manufacturing companies in South Carolina include BMW's automobile factory in

Tobacco is one of South Carolina's most important crops.

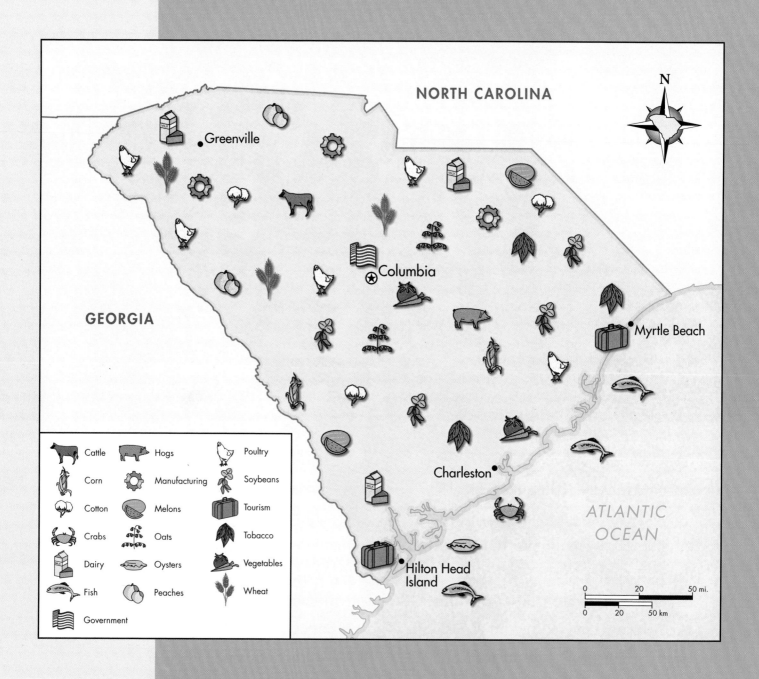

NORTH CAROLINA

GEORGIA

N

Greenville

Columbia

Myrtle Beach

Charleston

Hilton Head
Island

ATLANTIC
OCEAN

	Cattle		Hogs		Poultry
	Corn		Manufacturing		Soybeans
	Cotton		Melons		Tourism
	Crabs		Oats		Tobacco
	Dairy		Oysters		Vegetables
	Fish		Peaches		Wheat
	Government				

0   20   50 mi.

0   20   50 km

Greer, which employs many workers to produce its cars, and Deere and Company, which is well known for its agricultural and construction equipment.

The service industry accounts for a large part of South Carolina's employment and income. This industry includes businesses that perform a job or service for people, such as real estate, banking, healthcare, teaching, and managing stores and restaurants. Twenty-five of every hundred people in South Carolina hold service jobs. Columbia is the state's leading banking center. Seventeen of every one hundred people work for the state and federal governments. Many South Carolinians also work in jobs related to tourism, which is the business of providing food, shelter, and entertainment for visitors. Tourists spend almost $6 billion a year in the Palmetto State.

TAKE A TOUR OF SOUTH CAROLINA

South Carolina's beaches, golf courses, and historic sites lure millions of visitors to the state each year. From the Blue Ridge Mountains to the Atlantic Ocean, South Carolina offers stunning natural beauty for its citizens and visitors from around the globe.

The Coast

What better place to begin a tour of the Palmetto State than Charleston, where the state's history began. In 2000, the state's oldest city had a population of 96,650. A walk along the cobblestone streets takes you back

Horse-drawn carriages take visitors on a tour of historic Charleston.

in time. More than 600 buildings in the historic district were built before the 1800s. George Washington visited Charleston in 1791. He saw many of these same lovely homes and churches. The four clock faces in the steeple of St. Michael's Episcopal Church have been keeping time for the people of Charleston since 1764.

The historic district has mansions tucked away in side alleys. Some of these homes are hundreds of years old and were handed down through generations of family members. Charleston is also known for the "single house." These tall, narrow homes were built to take advantage of outside breezes during hot summers.

The Charleston Museum is the oldest museum in the United States. You'll find exhibits on slavery, the plantation system, and the Civil War. The Old Slave Mart stands as a haunting reminder of a time when slaves were bought and sold. The Slave Mart Museum offers presentations about the African-American experience in Charleston. Nearby is the Old Exchange building, built by the British in 1771. In its early days, the building served as a bustling place of business where taxes were paid on goods shipped and received. Later, during the Revolutionary War, a dungeon underneath the Exchange served as a prison.

This row of colorful homes in Charleston is referred to as Rainbow Row.

Cadets at the Citadel participate in precision drill practice.

On the banks of the Ashley River is The Citadel, a military college. It was originally founded to provide protection from slave rebellions for the city of Charleston. Today, almost two thousand students—both women and men—are enrolled at The Citadel. A museum on campus presents the history of the school from 1842 to the present.

About three miles (5 km) from downtown Charleston, history comes alive at the fort at Charles Towne Landing, site of the first English settlement of Charleston in 1670. You can learn all about the early colony by walking through a recreated village and touring a trading ship from the 1600s. Next, take a boat tour to Fort Sumter to see where the Civil War began and on to Fort Moultrie, site of the British attack during the American Revolution. At Charleston Harbor make one last stop at the South Carolina Aquarium. More than ten thousand animals live at the aquarium, including some that are rare and exotic.

FIND OUT MORE

Pawley's Island is one of the oldest beach resorts off the coast of South Carolina. This tiny island (only four miles long and a quarter mile wide at its widest point) is small on space but big on personality. The island is most famous for a legendary ghost called the Gray Man. Write your own ghost story about the Gray Man. Then find out what the real island legend is all about.

Some of the world's most beautiful gardens and plantations are in this area. At Cypress Gardens, you can paddle a boat through a cypress swamp. Magnolia Garden is the oldest major public garden in America. Middleton Place and Boone Hall, plantations from the 1700s, offer demonstrations of plantation life.

Beaufort, the state's second-oldest town, is fifty miles (80 km) south of Charleston. Beaufort is steeped in history. St. Helena's Episcopal Church was founded in 1712. Its tombstones served as operating tables during the Civil War. Several movies were filmed in this harbor town.

Nearby islands include St. Helena, Hunting, and Parris. Hunting Island State Park offers swimming, surfing, and fishing. For a view of the Atlantic Ocean and the surrounding islands, climb to the top of Hunting Island Lighthouse. The Parris Island Museum has exhibits ranging from the landing of the Spanish in 1521 to the marine recruit

Beaufort is a peaceful, historic town with majestic plantations and beautiful oak-lined roads.

training base. United States Marines have been stationed on Parris Island since 1891. Farther south are the popular family resorts of Kiawah Island and Hilton Head Island.

The "Grand Strand" refers to a sixty-mile (97-km) stretch of sparkling white beach along South Carolina's northern coast. The hub of the Grand Strand is Myrtle Beach. If you enjoy swimming, kite flying, and sand castle building, this is the place to visit. You can see wildlife of the wetlands and rare white albino alligators at Alligator Adventure. For a fun splash, try the water parks and slides.

Myrtle Beach is one of the most popular resorts on the East Coast.

Georgetown, site of the first English settlement in South Carolina, is on Winyah Bay. Exhibits at Georgetown's Rice Museum tell the story of the crop that helped make South Carolina rich.

The Midlands

The area between the coastal strip and the Piedmont is sometimes called the midlands. Much of the midlands was cotton country in the early

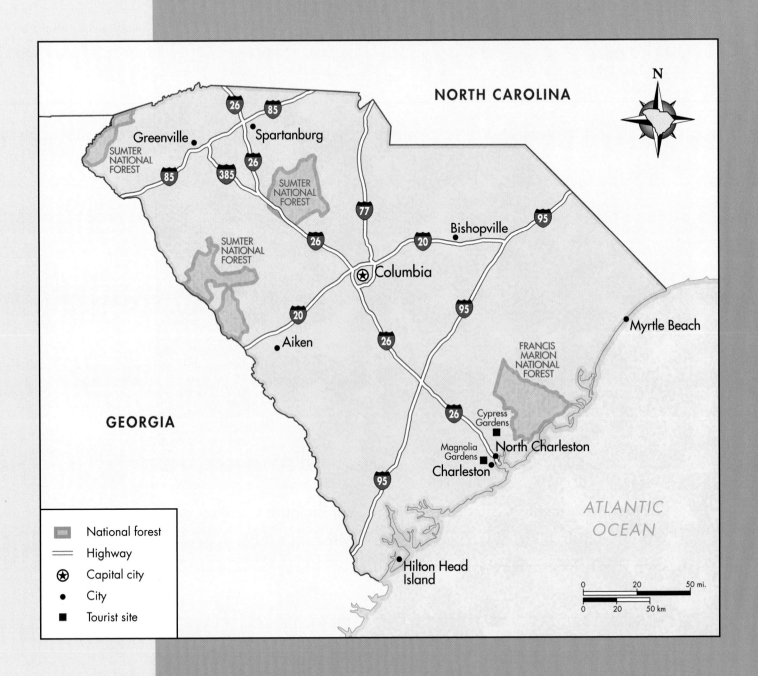

NORTH CAROLINA

N

Greenville

SUMTER
NATIONAL
FOREST

Spartanburg

SUMTER
NATIONAL
FOREST

SUMTER
NATIONAL
FOREST

Bishopville

Columbia

Aiken

GEORGIA

Myrtle Beach

FRANCIS
MARION
NATIONAL
FOREST

Cypress
Gardens

Magnolia
Gardens

North Charleston

Charleston

ATLANTIC
OCEAN

Hilton Head
Island

National forest

Highway

Capital city

City

Tourist site

0   20   50 mi.

0   20   50 km

1800s. Exhibits in the South Carolina Cotton Museum in Bishopville tell the story of cotton. Here you can see, smell, and feel cotton.

The Southern 500 stock-car race is held in Darlington every Labor Day weekend. Stock-cars are regular cars that have been turned into racing cars. Aiken hosts another kind of racing—horse racing. The annual Aiken Triple Crown attracts racing fans from all around the world.

Columbia, the capital city, is the only major city in the midlands. Not far from Columbia is the Congaree Swamp National Monument. Located next to the Congaree River, the Congaree swamp is an 11,000-acre (4,452-hectare) nature reserve. This is a great place to go canoeing, hiking, camping, and fishing. You can also take a guided tour of the swamp to get a good view of the many plants and animals living there, as well as some of the tallest trees in the eastern United States. Northeast of Columbia is Camden, home of the Carolina Cup. This popular horse racing event attracts more than 50,000 fans each year.

The Upcountry

The upcountry is a region of farmland, forests, mountains, modern industries, and historic towns. Rock Hill, in the far northern part of the state, has almost 50,000 residents. Scenes in the movie "The Patriot" were filmed in this area. At nearby Kings Mountain National Military Park, you can see exhibits related to the Revolutionary War battle. Also in the upcountry is Cowpens National Battlefield, with walking trails and exhibits.

Spartanburg, fifty miles (80 km) west of Rock Hill, was once a

Peaches have long been a staple of South Carolina's agriculture. Large-scale peach production began as far back as the 1860s. Today, South Carolina grows more peaches than any other state except California. Mouth-watering peach cobbler is a great way to enjoy this sweet and tasty fruit.

AUDREY'S PEACH COBBLER

8–10 cups of sliced peaches
1 cup of sugar
1 tablespoon of flour
1 tablespoon of butter
1 (8 oz.) can of Pillsbury Crescent Dinner Rolls©

1. Place the peaches in 9 x 13-inch baking dish.
2. Mix together sugar and flour. Pour over peaches.
3. Dot the top with butter.
4. Unroll the can of crescent rolls—do not separate the rolls.
5. Spread over top of peaches.
6. Bake at 300°F for 45 to 55 minutes.

At Cowpens National Battlefield you can watch a reenactment of this important Revolutionary War battle.

leading textile city. It is now home to many international companies. Stroll the streets of Spartanburg and you are likely to hear people speaking German, French, or Japanese. In spring, pink peach blossoms blanket the countryside.

Walnut Grove Plantation, near Roebuck, was the home of patriot heroine Kate Moore Barry. She served as a scout for the patriots during the Revolution. On one occasion, she received word that British raiders were in the area. Legend has it that since she had no one to care for her small daughter, she tied the child to a bedpost and rode off to warn her neighbors.

Looking for adventure? Take a ride in a zebra-striped bus at Hollywild Animal Park in Inman. Many of the park's animals have starred in movies and television commercials.

If you're interested in cars, check out the BMW Zentrum Museum at Greer. You'll find out how cars are manufactured, and see future car designs. You can even get a glimpse of James Bond 007's Z3 roadster from the movie "Goldeneye."

Greenville, once the hunting grounds of the Cherokee, is a fitting place to end a tour of the state. Greenville symbolizes South Carolina's devotion to the past while looking ahead to a very bright future. Downtown restoration projects are ongoing. The Poinsett Hotel, listed on the National Register of Historic Places, reopened in 2000 to its original 1925 grandeur. People of all ages enjoy downtown Greenville's street

The Reedy River runs through Greenville, one of South Carolina's largest cities.

festivals, music, sidewalk dining, international restaurants, theater —and of course, homemade ice cream.

Greenville carries on the age-old tradition of South Carolina's support of the arts. The Peace Center for the Performing Arts, the Greenville County Museum of Art, community theaters, Furman University, and Bob Jones University, the largest fundamentalist Christian school in the United States, offer varied cultural opportunities. The Bob Jones Art Gallery houses one of the largest collections of religious art in America.

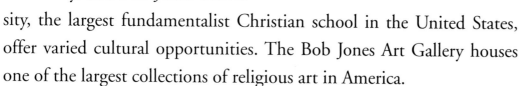

A worker at the BMW factory puts the finishing touches on a car.

Greenville County's population has grown from 288,000 to almost 380,000 in the past twenty years. Companies such as BMW, Michelin, and Hitachi have brought in workers from other places. Along with growth comes more industry, new homes, and new schools.

The Greenville Grrrowl, a minor-league hockey team, plays at the Bi-Lo Arena. Nearby Clemson University draws thousands of Greenville residents to football games. Greenville also has a playground in its own backyard—the Blue Ridge Mountains.

It's no wonder that South Carolina's scenic beauty, rich history, and friendly people attract so many visitors each year.

SOUTH CAROLINA ALMANAC

Statehood date and number: May 23, 1788; 8th

State seal: On the left side of the oval-shaped state seal is a drawing of a palmetto tree standing over an uprooted oak. On the right is a figure of hope holding a laurel branch with the sun rising behind her. Adopted in 1776.

State flag: The blue flag has a silver palmetto tree in the center. It also features a silver crescent shaped like a quarter moon in the upper left corner.

Geographic center: Richland, 13 miles (21 km) southeast of Columbia

Total area/rank: 32,007 square miles (82,898 sq km)/40th

Coastline: 300 miles (483 km)

Borders: North Carolina, Georgia, and the Atlantic Ocean

Latitude and longitude: Approximately between 32° 04' and 35° 12' N and 78° 31' and 83° 23' W

Highest/lowest elevation: Sassafras Mountain 3,560 feet (1,085 m)/Atlantic Ocean, sea level

Hottest/coldest temperature: 111°F (44°C) in June 1954 at Camden/–20°F (–29°C) in January 1977 at Caesar's Head

Land area/rank: 30,111 square miles (77,987 sq km)/40th

Inland water area: 1,006 square miles (2,606 sq km)

Population/rank: 4,012,012/26th (2000 Census)

Population of major cities:

Columbia: 116, 278

Charleston: 96,650

North Charleston: 79,641

Greenville: 56,002

Spartanburg: 39,673

Origin of state name: First called *Carolana* in honor of Charles I. Called *Carolina* in charter of 1663 issued by Charles II. The area was later divided into South Carolina and North Carolina.

State capital: Columbia

Previous capital: Charleston

Counties: 46

State government: 46 senators, 124 representatives

Major rivers, lakes: Pee Dee, Santee, Broad, Saluda, Savannah Rivers/ Lake Marion, Lake Moultrie

Farm products: Tobacco, soybeans, corn, wheat, cotton, and peaches, milk, and eggs

Livestock: Cattle, hogs, chickens, and turkeys

Manufactured products: Chemicals, textiles, machinery, paper and paper products, rubber and plastic products

Mining products: Granite and limestone

Fishing products: Crabs, shrimp, oysters, and clams

Animal: White-tailed deer

Beverage: Milk

Bird: Carolina Wren

Butterfly: Eastern Tiger Swallowtail

Dance: Shag

Dog: Boykin Spaniel

Flower: Yellow Jessamine

Fruit: Peach

Game bird: Wild turkey

Gem: Amethyst

Insect: Carolina mantid

Mottos: *Animis opibusque parati* (Prepared in mind and resources) and *Dum spiro spero* (While I breathe, I hope)

Nickname: Palmetto State

Reptile: Loggerhead sea turtle

Shell: Lettered Olive

Song: "Carolina" by Henry Timrod, music by Anne Custis Burgess. Adopted in 1911.

Stone: Blue Granite

Tree: Palmetto Tree

Wildlife: Deer, black bears, wildcats, raccoons, foxes, squirrels, rabbits, rattlesnakes, water moccasins, ducks, doves, egrets, herons, mockingbirds, wrens, sparrows, bluebirds, and pelicans

TIME**LINE**

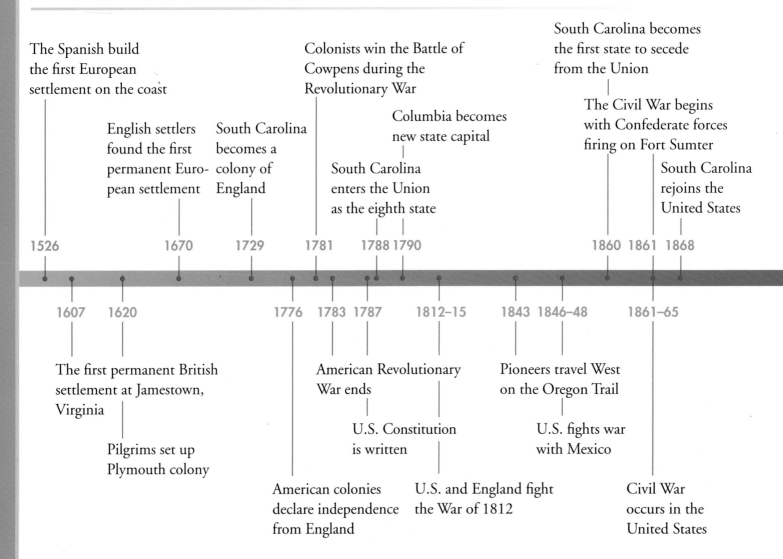

The Spanish build the first European settlement on the coast

English settlers found the first permanent European settlement

South Carolina becomes a colony of England

Colonists win the Battle of Cowpens during the Revolutionary War

Columbia becomes new state capital

South Carolina enters the Union as the eighth state

South Carolina becomes the first state to secede from the Union

The Civil War begins with Confederate forces firing on Fort Sumter

South Carolina rejoins the United States

1526   1670   1729   1781   1788 1790   1860 1861 1868

1607 1620   1776 1783 1787   1812–15   1843 1846–48   1861–65

The first permanent British settlement at Jamestown, Virginia

Pilgrims set up Plymouth colony

American Revolutionary War ends

U.S. Constitution is written

American colonies declare independence from England

Pioneers travel West on the Oregon Trail

U.S. fights war with Mexico

U.S. and England fight the War of 1812

Civil War occurs in the United States

UNITED STATES **HISTORY**

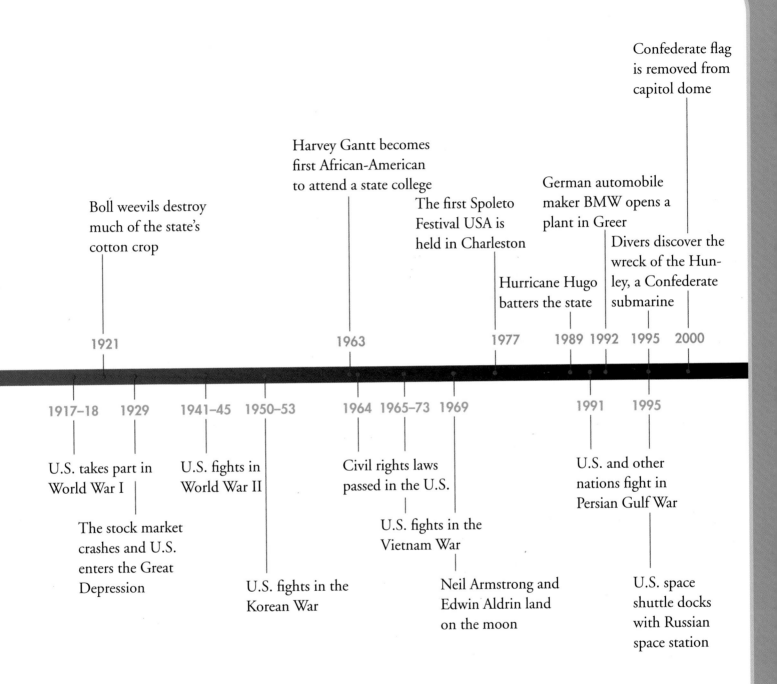

Boll weevils destroy much of the state's cotton crop

Harvey Gantt becomes first African-American to attend a state college

The first Spoleto Festival USA is held in Charleston

German automobile maker BMW opens a plant in Greer

Confederate flag is removed from capitol dome

Hurricane Hugo batters the state

Divers discover the wreck of the Hunley, a Confederate submarine

1921   1963   1977   1989 1992 1995 2000

1917–18 1929   1941–45 1950–53   1964 1965–73 1969   1991   1995

U.S. takes part in World War I

U.S. fights in World War II

Civil rights laws passed in the U.S.

U.S. and other nations fight in Persian Gulf War

The stock market crashes and U.S. enters the Great Depression

U.S. fights in the Vietnam War

U.S. fights in the Korean War

Neil Armstrong and Edwin Aldrin land on the moon

U.S. space shuttle docks with Russian space station

GALLERY OF FAMOUS SOUTH CAROLINIANS

Mary McLeod Bethune
(1875–1955)
Educator and leader of the African-American community. She founded the National Council of Negro Women, and served as special advisor on minority affairs to President Franklin Roosevelt. Grew up in Mayesville.

James Dickey
(1923–1997)
Well-known writer who gained fame for his poems and stories of the South. Born in Georgia and lived in Columbia.

Dizzy Gillespie
(1917–1993)
Famous jazz trumpeter and composer. Many of his compositions, including "Night in Tunisia," became jazz classics. Born in Cheraw.

Angelina and Sarah Grimké
(1805–1879) (1792–1873)
Abolitionists and supporters of women's rights. The sisters were among the first women in the country to become well known public speakers. Born in Charleston.

Thomas Heyward
(1746–1809)
Served in the Continental Congress and signed the Declaration of Independence. Born in St. Luke's Parish.

Andrew Jackson
(1767–1845)
Politician. Seventh president of the United States. Born in Waxhaw.

Jasper Johns
(1930–)
Painter. Leader in the pop art movement. Born in Allendale.

Eartha Kitt
(1928–)
Internationally known singer and actress who has appeared on the stage, on television, and on film. Born in North.

Robert Smalls
(1839–1915)
Born a slave in Beaufort, Smalls became a Civil War hero for the Union navy. Also served as a United States congressman.

GLOSSARY

census: an official counting of population

colony: a group of people living in a new land while being governed by their native country

constitution: the basic laws and principles under which a country, state, or organization is governed

controversy: a public dispute

economy: the management of resources, such as money, materials, and labor

fall line: an imaginary line joining waterfalls on a series of rivers and marking the farthest point inland where river-going boats can travel

gorge: deep, narrow passage with steep, rocky sides, often with a stream flowing through it

Great Depression: hard economic times of the United States during the 1930s

heritage: a tradition; something that is passed down through many generations

international: involving two or more nations

invention: something new that was produced or created by a person using their imagination

National Register of Historic Places: a list of important people and events that have shaped the history of the United States

piedmont: at the foot of the mountain

plantation: a large farm, usually requiring many workers

precipitation: rain, snow, or sleet

rebel: person who resists or defies an authority

rebellion: opposition toward a government or authority

revolution: uprising against a government; a complete change in government or rule

rural: areas that are associated with the country

segregation: the practice of separating a particular race or class of people from another, such as in housing or schools

slave: a person who is owned by and forced to work for someone else

stock-car: a standard car that has been made into a racing car

textile: fiber, yarn, or cloth

tourism: the business of providing food, shelter, and entertainment for visitors

FOR MORE INFORMATION

Web sites

State of South Carolina
http://www.myscgov.com
Official web site for South Carolina state government.

South Carolina Department of Parks, Recreation, and Tourism
http://www.travelsc.com
Provides travel information and facts about South Carolina.

South Carolina Aquarium
http://www.scaquarium.org
Includes photographs and information about the aquarium.

Southern Festivals Newspaper
http://www.southfest.com
Provides information, dates, and locations for festivals in South Carolina and other southern states.

Books

Colbert, Nancy A. *The Firing on Fort Sumter: A Splintered Nation Goes to War.* Morgan Reynolds, 2001.

Cornelius, Kay and Arthur Meier Schlesinger. *Francis Marion: The Swamp Fox (Revolutionary War Leaders).* Chelsea House Publishing, 2000.

Fradin, Dennis Brindell. *The South Carolina Colony.* Danbury, CT: Children's Press, 1992.

Russell, Ching Yeung. *A Day on a Shrimp Boat.* Columbia, SC: Sandlapper Publishing Company, 1993.

Addresses

Office of the Governor
P.O. Box 11829
Columbia, SC 29211

South Carolina Department of Parks, Recreation, and Tourism
PO Box 71
Columbia, SC 29202

INDEX

ABOUT THE AUTHOR

Myra S. Weatherly grew up on a farm in upstate South Carolina. After having lived in other parts of the United States, she has now returned to her roots. Research for this book involved traveling to her favorite haunts and some new places, too. She also used library resources, surfed the Internet, and talked with many people, including old-timers, newcomers, and visitors to the state.

The author's published works include magazine articles and books for children and young adults. Myra holds a bachelor's degree in English and a master's degree in gifted education. She also makes school visits and conducts workshops for teachers and writers.